nF419167

IF I
HAD A
DAUGHTER

IF I HAD A DAUGHTER

Pearls of Wisdom for Young Women

ZOE-ANN BARTLETT

This book is for Isabella . . .
the daughter I never had

and

For Madelyn, who embodies the beauty,
love, and possibility I see for this world

This book is inspired by
one simple truth—

*our individual journey in
this life is the sum of
our choices*

The offerings here are intended to
help escort a positive journey . . . or
at least avoid a few pitfalls.

What choices will you make?

Contents

Introduction

For many years, my mom was a single mom, partly due to my father's isolated tours of duty required by the Air Force. When he returned from Vietnam in 1970, our family was transferred from Maine to New Mexico. Shortly after this transfer, their marriage dissolved. Mom was left to support my brother and me in a different part of the country, where she knew no one, suffered tremendously from a permanent and ruthless back injury from her youth, and received no support from my father. Despite her hardships, she was an amazing mom; she encouraged us, believed in us, supported our interests, laughed with us, and loved us deeply.

As excellent a mom as she was, she *never* told me to moisturize my neck! How could she not tell me the importance of this act? At fifteen, I was trying desperately to suck every possible ounce of moisture from my face to prevent pimples! I never knew I should take care to moisturize my neck. Not until my late forties did I understand the consequences of this valuable lesson. So naturally, this was the first thing I promised to teach my daughter, if I had one. And that is how these "pearls of wisdom" began.

I hope this book becomes an heirloom to pass on generationally: from mothers to daughters, mentors to mentees, aunties to nieces, older friends to younger ones. This collection contains empty pages at the end of each section to write additional lessons to encourage the book's passage from woman to woman.

Inevitably, life teaches us little gems of wisdom through our own experiences to share throughout our lifetime. Some are humorous, and some are profound. All are worth consideration.

I want this book to spark thought and consideration for how you can grow into a dynamic and confident woman, while avoiding some of the hidden pitfalls that arise from the choices we make in our younger years. In truth though, many (if not most) of these insights are suitable for women of all ages. After all, it's never too late to make positive changes in our lives, right? Right!

Life's experience has been my teacher, in addition to my mom, mentors, friends, and wise "aunties."

Here's to Woman Power! May we all support and inspire each other to live the brightest, healthiest, and happiest life possible.

*Tell me, what
is it you plan
to do with
your wild and
precious life?*

MARY OLIVER

I would teach her there are a few non-negotiable values for living your best *Life*.

Consider these your magic bullets for a positive life. These are the foundational elements to invite health and happiness into your life. You have only *one* life on this sweet earth. Make it count!

Live a BIG life. It's why you are on this earth.

Live your life with 100% responsibility. *You* are in charge. The cumulative results of the choices you've made and will make create your life's experience. Choose well.

Demonstrate self-respect. If you don't show it to yourself, who will?

Know how to be alone, content, and peaceful with yourself.

Practice gratitude. This practice, while seemingly simple, has the secret power of a magical pill. It is the antithesis of entitlement and the balm of contentment.

Don't smoke. Don't vape. Period.

YOU ARE ENOUGH.

For You

*Love is a verb.
Love—the feeling—
is the fruit of love,
the verb.*

*So love her:
Serve her. Sacrifice.
Listen to her.
Empathize.
Appreciate.
Affirm her.*

I would teach her the importance of and different forms of *Love*.

The value of love in life is fundamental. It is the most important indicator of happiness and a driver of being a compassionate human being. True love is unconditional and is shown through kindness, patience, and humility with *all* living things. However, you must extend love to yourself first, then others. Perhaps the trickiest is romantic love, though there are many ways to establish healthy partnerships for a long-lasting love story.

IT IS THE MOST IMPORTANT INDICATOR OF HAPPINESS & A DRIVER OF BEING A COMPASSIONATE HUMAN BEING

LOVE
of
OTHERS

Develop *conversational* and *active* listening skills. It is imperative to not be self-centered.

Curiosity is your map. Your navigation tools are understanding the three levels of listening:

LEVEL 1: *Focused on yourself and your reactions*

You are caught up in your own thoughts, opinions, feelings, and judgements. This level is good for collecting information or when facing a decision.

LEVEL 2: *Focused on the other person*

Your attention is on another and you pay attention to what is being said, how it is said, the body language. You choose how to respond given this information.

LEVEL 3: *Focused on another and the context of their environment*

This is where the juice is. Some call it the third vault. A level 3 listener hears what is said but is also attuned to what is not said. This is the deepest form of effective listening, which leads to richer and deeper conversations.

Recommended reading: *4 Essential Keys to Effective Communication in Love, Life, Work - Anywhere!* by Bento C. Leal III

KIND
Towards
OT

NESS
HERS

Speak your truth but find a way to do it from a place of love. Communication without love can cause heartache, misunderstanding, and bitterness.

There is no value in blame. It takes away energy. Instead, choose to be curious. This will help you to respond, not react.

Recognize that *intention* and *impact* are different.

Recommended reading:
The 5 Love Languages
by Gary Chapman

GIVE TO Others

Practice yoga. Yoga means union—the union of your body and mind with a greater, more universal consciousness.

Write thank you notes. They make people feel good, and they acknowledge the thoughtfulness others have shown you and demonstrate your gratitude.

Give gifts with nothing expected in return.

Show respect, particularly to those older than you. Others have seen and experienced more than you can imagine.

Ask your parents about their lives pre-you. They once had their own youth and stories. This will allow you the gift of knowing them better as people, not just by the role they play in your life.

Respect and cherish your friends. They are your chosen family.

Your circle of friends will change as you and your interests change. Learn that friends are in your life for a reason, a season, or a lifetime. Accepting this lesson will save you much heartache when things begin to shift.

Watch the movie *Steel Magnolias*. You will understand the value of girlfriends and their impact on all aspects of life. Bring tissues.

romantic RELATIONSHIPS

It takes courage to love in this world . . . go for as much as you can hold. Love is worth it.

Words and actions must match in relationships. Follow through.

Demonstrate enthusiastic and compassionate presence with others. Don't you want the same?

Learn how to be in healthy conflict.

Avoid:
- Defensiveness
- Contempt
- Stonewalling
- Criticism

When you enter a romantic relationship, maintain a balance between your own interests, your friendships, and your new special someone. This balance will help prevent losing yourself. It's easy to do, especially in a new relationship.

Recommended reading:
The Seven Principles for Making Marriage Work
by John Gottman

SEX and
INTIMACY

It's normal to be curious.

Sexuality and *sensuality* are different. Sensuality is being aware, accepting, and comfortable with your own body before you share it with another.

Intimacy takes two. It is the ability to share emotional closeness with another human being and have it returned.

Your body, your rules.

If your parents don't talk with you about sex (and many don't), find someone or a source you trust to do so. Sex and sexuality are a normal and healthy part of our lives!

Enjoy sexual expression, arousal, and orgasm without fear, guilt, or shame.

Use protection.

Consent is paramount, then have fun!

Recommended Instagram following: Nicole_thesexprofessor, University of Washington

COMMITTED & ENDURING *Relationships*

Consider not marrying until you're *thirty*—this gives you time to know who you are and discern what you want.

You must be the one before you find the one.

You do not need anyone to "complete" you.

Before you say yes, ask this of yourself: would you elope with your partner with no fanfare and not regret it? If the answer is no, question your motives. Perhaps you are more motivated by the wedding than the marriage.

Think of enduring relationships as beautiful gardens. They weather the seasons over the years, and to do so, they need constant care to thrive each year. They must be watered, weeded, cultivated, and tended. Otherwise, the weeds will take over, and plants will perish.

For You

When you are
sorrowful look
again in your
heart, and you
shall see that in
truth you are
weeping for that
which has been
your delight.

KAHLIL GIBRAN

I would teach her that part of living is *Dying.*

This subject can be scary to learn and talk about. It sometimes spurs our greatest fears, anxiety, and sadness. The antidote is opening up and talking about your feelings with friends, family, counselors, or support groups.

THERE ARE RESOURCES OUT THERE. WHEN THE TIME COMES, USE THEM.

Letting GO

Your first experience with death (an inevitable part of life) can be scary. It's one of life's most difficult experiences. Undoubtedly, you will have many questions and a lot of feelings. This is okay and natural.

You will go through a range of emotions (anger, sadness, relief, among others) maybe even for a long time. Feel what you feel. Talk about what you are experiencing with those who don't tell you how to feel, but who *listen*. Just don't keep it bottled up inside.

It's helpful to think about grief as a loop and not a line. There is no clean start or finish line, where grief begins and ends. Your process will not be the same as anyone else's.

Remember, it won't feel like this forever.

For you and others, remember that grief is a gradual process. It is to be expected, and it is okay.

You have your life ahead of you, but that doesn't mean when milestones occur (graduations, birthdays, marriage) that you won't especially miss your loved one and feel grief in conjunction with happiness. It can be confusing. Consider finding a creative way to honor the person's memory and contribute to the joy of the occasion. The person you love would want that for you.

YOUR PART

Sometimes receiving "permission" is necessary for the person who is dying. When it comes time to say goodbye to a dying loved one, these simple words may help them (and you):

- I love you.
- I will miss you.
- I will be okay.
- It is okay to go.

It is a privilege and an honor to witness a person through the process of leaving this planet. It is also one of the hardest things you will ever do.

Help those you love by being prepared for your passing when you become an adult. Have these four key documents to protect yourself and those you love:

- A living revocable trust
- A will
- An advance directive and durable power of attorney for health care
- A financial power of attorney

It is helpful to leave a list of accounts and passwords for the person who will settle your estate.

For You

Education is the most powerful weapon which you can use to change the world.

I would teach her that *Learning* is a noble lifelong pursuit.

School is only one medium of education. There are many others.

Our universe is expansive with cultures, languages, history, space, undersea exploration, nature, art, hobbies, and endless subjects to explore.

HOW
LEAR

Approach learning with a sense of awe by cultivating curiosity and then following where it leads.

It is essential to be a critical thinker and discern fact from fiction, which takes skill and practice. Not always easy in the world of social media. Do try, though, to be informed and open, not cynical and judgmental.

Have a blast finding things that pique your interest and open your mind.

Read.
READ.
READ.

Data + knowledge = information
Data + knowledge + context =
understanding, empowerment,
& wisdom

Ask good questions. You will learn much from listening.

Set goals, but don't stop there! Make sure to set up systems to help you meet your goals . . . this is where you will find the magic.

At some point, take one year to travel and experience the world. Travel changes everything. Your perspective will broaden through cultural awareness, ways to live, history, and so much more. You'll be more interesting and develop more of a worldview.

Celebrate your successes and your defeats. Defeats often teach us more.

Recommended reading:
Atomic Habits
by James Clear

CONFLICT, ANGER, RESOLU

and TION

Please, I beg you, refrain from using "I'm sorry" as a default response! Save it for when you really mean it.

Focus on the solution—not the problem you are trying to solve. What do you want to create?

When expressing your views and options, know your data and cite your sources. Then be willing to listen without judgment to other perspectives. (I know, not always easy to do).

Respond only to what you know, not to what could or might happen. Worrying is a waste of energy.

Judging others negatively is easy to do. But it may not serve you. Everyone has an unknown backstory.

Choose
PEACE

Send love from your heart—even if you are angry. Yes, *love*!

Try this sometime: when someone cuts you off on the road, instead of flipping the bird, send them love. By doing so, you diffuse anger and escalation.

THINK BEFORE YOU SPEAK

Cultivate the ability to forgive yourself and others, when necessary.

Learn to manage anger and use it productively. A few tips:

1. Give yourself a bit of time before expressing yourself.
2. Use "I statements" instead of "you statements."
3. Physical activity, time in nature, and meditation help calm and restore a peaceful and loving heart.
4. Humor can help diffuse a heated encounter, however, be careful not to use sarcasm. That will only make things worse.

EXPAND your
PERSPECTIVE

Study a second language from a young age and find ways to practice it. Even if you are older, it's never too late.

Consider playing chess. It will teach you to think critically.

Learn how to cook a favorite recipe, and share it with others.

Play at least one sport. Learning constructive competition, team dynamics, and how to find your own personal best will help you build confidence.

If you love music and want to play an instrument, consider one you can play throughout your life. Piano or guitar is the most timeless.

Teach by letting others do—otherwise, they may not learn.

Discover friends of *all* ages. The richness and texture make life more enjoyable.

For You

Beauty is the illumination of your soul.

JOHN O'DONOHUE

If I had a daughter . . .

I would teach her that *Beauty* is rich in meaning and that having confidence and grace is paramount.

YOUR *Essence*

You will be amazed at how the universe responds in kind when you demonstrate welcoming and happy energy.

Graciously receive compliments when they are given. Simply say "thank you." Stop yourself from making excuses or devaluing yourself.

Look for the good and beautiful in all things. You are the architect of your own thoughts. What will you build?

Confidence is beautiful in women. It radiates strength, self-awareness, and conviction. It shows you trust yourself.

Find one beautiful thing each day that leaves you with a sense of awe. Hint: consider using a "wonder journal" to capture and remember them.

Ask yourself this question often: what can soften? Is it perhaps the rigidity of your schedule? The tone of your voice? Your choice of words or point of view?

Laughter before bed is good medicine.

Consider writing love letters or a card to yourself periodically. It's a powerful tool to draw out your inner wisdom and show yourself compassion.

PHYSI

BE

CAL
AUTY

Moisturize your *neck*, not just your face! You will not understand this until you are in your forties. This is the lesson that started them all for me. Nora Ephron hadn't yet made this sentiment famous in her book, *I Feel Bad About My Neck*. It goes to show, it's an important lesson!

Wear sunscreen on your face, neck, chest, and forearms every day, rain or shine. It will pay off in later years.

Be conscious of your posture. It reflects your self-esteem.

Floss your teeth. Every day.

Be comfortable and confident with or without makeup. It's essential to love yourself and let the true beauty of your inner light always shine.

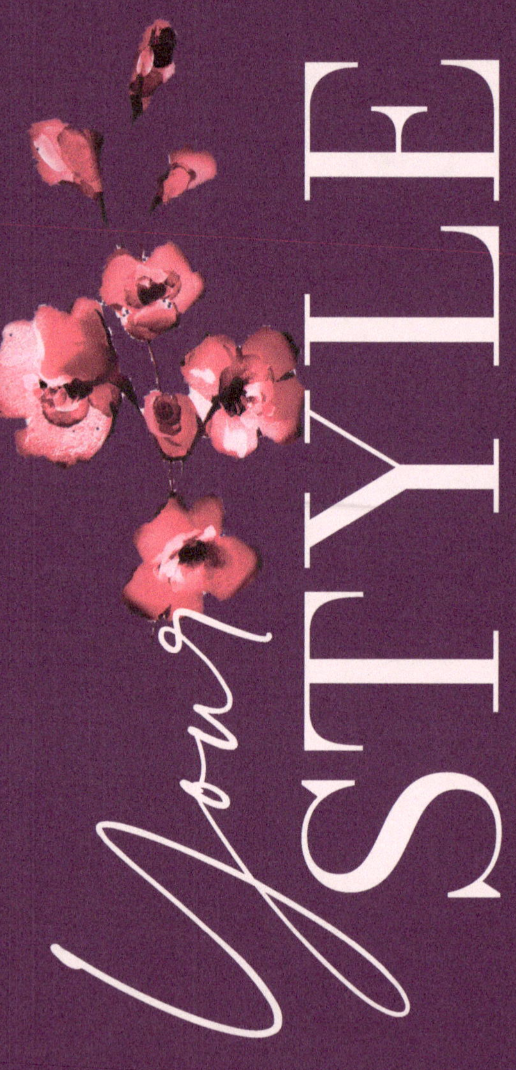
Your
STYLE

Consider the construct of your body type. With this knowledge, you will understand the clothing styles that look best on you and help you develop your personal brand.

Build a wardrobe based on basics, the right colors for your skin type. Then accessorize. This will save you endless aggravation and an enormous amount of money throughout your lifetime.

Understand the importance of etiquette. This is a life skill that shows kindness, consideration, and humility. It can help you in business and distinguish you in relationships.

For You

Home is what you take with you, not what you leave behind.

N.K. JEMISIN

I would teach
her what
Home really means.

You'll likely have many homes in your lifetime, those you share with your family as you grow up and those you'll have as you begin new chapters of your own life. Eventually, you might choose to buy your own home.

Recognize home is where you live, both in *spirit* and *place*.

Live where your heart soars and you find inspiration.

Keep your load light. Consumption is not a pathway to happiness or fulfillment.

PEACE

There are three essential pieces of furniture:

1. A comfy place to read. This spot is where you will travel great distances with your mind, heart, and soul.
2. A desk, even if it is makeshift. And have access to a computer. From here, you will dream, create, and plan.
3. A dining table. Fill the chairs around your table often with those you love and those you'd like to know better. Food nourishes the body and the soul.

Bring only things you love into your home.

Regardless if you rent or buy, consider placing written blessings of close friends and family under your rugs, behind photos or something else creative. You will feel the love of those who care about you, even when you are alone.

Choose your home in the dead of winter when nature pulls back the curtain and you can see more clearly. It might be surprising what you'll find and if you'll still want the home after what you see. If it passes the winter test, you'll love the house for a long time, in all seasons.

For You

With every experience, you alone are painting your own canvas, thought by thought, choice by choice.

OPRAH WINFREY

I would teach her a few *Practical* things about day-to-day living.

We live in a busy society and world, with endless elements competing for our time and attention. As you get older and take on responsibilities such as managing money, living on your own, and starting your career, the following points to make your life easier.

DAILY
Living

There is an order of operations to daily living. Ask yourself: what is the *next best action* to take? (Especially helpful when you feel a bit overwhelmed.)

Follow through on what you say you will do. If you cannot do something that is asked of you, negotiate. Your word is your bond.

Measure twice and cut once. Always.

Develop organizational skills and support mechanisms that work for you. Having these systems in place will declutter your mind. They will also help structure your thinking and your life.

Prepar

Know how to change a tire. This may save your life one day.

Have a disaster-ready kit, appropriate for geographic location, in your home and car. The peace of mind is invaluable, and we owe it to those we love.

Know what to do and where to go in an emergency (car accident, fire, hospital, earthquake, whatever). Then live your life without fear.

Know where the shut-off valve is for your home's water main and how to turn off the gas main.

Develop good knife skills (with good knives) in the kitchen. Cooking will be more enjoyable, faster, and safer.

Math and Excel are your friends. These essential tools come in handy in school, work, and play.

Grow a tomato plant (or vegetable of some kind) in a pot or garden each summer. It's a good reminder food is a work of nature and not something to be taken for granted.

Try to eat and shop locally. You will make less of an imprint on the earth and support the community you live in.

MONEY

Understand money. No need to fear it; it's part of life.

Live simply and beneath your means. It prevents tremendous stress and opens the doors of possibility.

Save. Buy what you want when you can pay for it without using credit. If used unwisely, credit is a burden and can cost you your freedom.

Understand the value of tracking, compounding, savings, and 401(k)s. Your money is your responsibility, not anyone else's.

Know how to read a balance sheet, cash flow statement, and profit and loss statement. Also, know how to write a budget.

Educate yourself about investing, even if you work with an advisor.

Recommended reading:
The Soul of Money
by Lynne Twist &
Teresa Barker

If you don't know where to start, read, watch, or listen to the advice of financial advisor Suze Orman

Profess

Beginning in your youth, spend time with women of different professions. These experiences will help expand and inspire your own life's work.

Measure yourself by your character, not by your job title or income.

Give clear expectations. Then acknowledge and appreciate work done for you by others.

Express yourself with confidence. People want you to be successful and authentic. For example, if you're giving a presentation, tell a story—don't read the slides, for goodness sake!

Limit your alcohol consumption to two drinks per event, particularly in a professional setting.

Form a personal team of professionals you trust (doctor, financial advisor, lawyer, and anyone else you need).

PETS

Be kind to animals. This kindness is a measure of your character.

Consider getting a pet only when you don't have to leave the animal by itself all day.

Train your animal (with kindness and consistency, of course). English isn't your animal's first language! Remember: there are bad owners, but not bad animals.

Oh, and don't forget to pick up the poop!

If you are outgrowing who you've been, you are right on schedule. Keep evolving.

LALAH DELIA

For You

Enjoy a happy life!

I LOVE YOU.

About the Author

Zoe-Ann Bartlett is a successful entrepreneur, having founded Intentional Table, LLC, Love Tiny Bubbles, and Wink Cupcakes, a boutique catering company. She's been a contributing writer to *Living Luxe* magazine with travel articles on Washington State wines and the Kentucky Bourbon Trail. As a lifelong learner, Zoe-Ann completed a culinary internship program in France, as well as her Bachelor of Science from Texas Tech University. Additional studies include Level 1 Sommelier, through the International Sommelier Guild; coaching training program with the Co-Active Institute; and a 200-hour certificate from the Yoga Alliance. Zoe-Ann also co-taught "How to Start a Small Food Business" at North and South Seattle Community Colleges. In her early career, Zoe-Ann led the Global Travel Management program for Expedia and Microsoft Corporation, earning numerous accolades and awards for her work in the travel and hospitality industries. Many of her early years were with Marriott Hotels and Resorts, where her passion for hospitality, food and wine, travel, and architecture merged. She is an avid yoga practitioner, traveler, and lover of Jack Russell terriers.

There are many things in life that will catch your eye, but only a few will catch your heart. Pursue those.

MICHAEL NOLAN